W9-CBX-386

FAMOUS AMERICAN WOMEN

Famous American Heroes and Leaders Series:

Founders of Fortunes, Book One

Founders of Fortunes, Book Two

Founders of Our Cities

Citizens Born Abroad

Explorers of Our Land

Heroes in Time of War

Crusaders for a Cause

Famous American Women

Famous American Negroes

Famous American Indians

FAMOUS AMERICAN WOMEN

by

L. EDMOND LEIPOLD, Ph.D.

Publishers

T. S. DENISON & COMPANY, INC.

Minneapolis

First Printing—November 1967
Second Printing—April 1968
Third Printing—August 1968
Fourth Printing—December 1968

Printed in the U.S.A.
BY THE BRINGS PRESS

Library of Congress Catalog Card Number: 67-24773

Dedication

TO MY FIVE CALIFORNIA GRANDDAUGHTERS

Foreword

America has been called the great melting pot of the world, for to its shores came men, women, and children of all nations and creeds and races. What our great nation is today is the sum total of the contributions of these many people. Included among the founders and builders of our country are many women, for they, too, assumed their full share of responsibility in the making of America. In this book are the life stories of ten of these women, each of whom added her share to the nation's greatness. One was a heroine of a battlefield, another guided two of our most famous explorers through a wild and dangerous region, another wrote beautiful poetry. Each in her own way added her contribution to America's illustrious history.

L.E.L.

Contents

Willa Cather

Pioneer Village Author

In the prairie state of Nebraska is a town with the unusual name of Red Cloud. It is a small town, typical of the many others like it in the Middle West. Past it flows the Republican River, its waters on their way to join the "Big Muddy" Missouri to the east.

When Red Cloud was but a tiny frontier village, a man named Charles Cather moved to a farm nearby, close to the Kansas border. He had seven children, one of whom bore the pretty name of Willa. They had come to Red Cloud because the father's brother and father had moved there.

Their previous home was near Winchester in the beautiful Shenandoah Valley of Virginia. To the east of their farm the brooding Blue Ridge Mountains loomed high, their forest-covered crests seeming to cover half the sky. It was a good valley, but Charles Cather felt hemmed in. He heard that Nebraska was big and flat, where one could see the horizon many miles in the distance. It was the year 1882, when Willa was nine years old, that they left their lovely valley home to move to the Western frontier town.

Red Cloud was in a region that was still in its infancy. Only six years before this, General George Custer and all of his men had been wiped out in a fierce battle with the Indians on the Montana border to the northwest. The number of settlers was still small and life was hard for those who braved the hot summers and the fierce arctic winters to make their homes there.

Willa was not happy about the change, especially at first. She had spent the first years of her childhood in the mountainous Virginia country which was so different from the land about her new home. Gradually she learned to love the prairie about her. There was an appeal about it that grew with the passing of time. She loved to ride horseback and she had her own pony to take her on many wonderful jaunts about the countryside. She soon knew well the neighborhood about her and the names of the families that lived on the widely scattered farms. Many of them had recently migrated to America from lands across the ocean, and Willa liked to visit with them and to hear about the countries across the sea. The prairie was big and the space wide about her, every mile of which she learned to love.

During the several years that she lived on the farm, Willa had the opportunity to get but little "book learning," but the experiences that she had more than made up for the lack of schooling. When the Cathers moved into the village of Red Cloud, Willa enrolled in the little high school that had been established there and at once showed herself to be a capable student. The farm years had not been wasted, for Willa had spent many hours reading good literature during the time the family had made their home on the open prairie, and now she profited from her self-study. Her teachers were impressed by her ability and took pains to help her in every way possible. It is interesting to note that as long as forty years after she left school she was still writing regularly to her former high school principal.

At the time she was in high school she was the type of girl who stood out in her group. She was pretty, with hair as short as a boy's, and she preferred to dress in blue jeans rather than skirts. This was in the 1880's, long before short hair and jeans were common girls' costumes. Instead of spending her time in such girlish pursuits as cooking and sewing, she much preferred to ride her pony into the country, there to camp out on the prairie and to revel in the natural beauty about her. In later years, after she had become a famous author, she often drew upon these experiences to work them into the story plots.

Upon finishing high school she went to Lincoln, Nebraska's capital city, where she enrolled at the state university. She had no idea at this time of taking up writing as her life's work, but enrolled in a premedical course to prepare her for a career as a doctor. It wasn't long before her talent as a writer became apparent, and a number of her articles were published in the university magazine. Gradually she lost interest in the medical course that she was taking, being attracted more and more toward a writing career. By the time she was a sophomore it was almost certain in which field her primary interest lay.

Willa now began contributing regularly to the **Nebraska State Journal**, receiving a dollar for each column she wrote. She liked this kind of activity, but was seldom satisfied with her efforts. It is apparent now that this experience was very valuable to her, aiding her to develop an individual style of writing that attracted many readers.

Upon finishing college, she returned to her home town of Red Cloud, but found life there to be aimless and dull. There was little or nothing there to keep her occupied and she decided that her best course of action would be to seek employment elsewhere. When a magazine called **The Home Monthly** began publication in Pittsburgh, Pennsylvania, its editor had taken note of her ability as a writer and offered her a position on the staff. Willa was only too glad to accept the offer, leaving Red Cloud at once. The work was interesting and pleasing to her, but when a newspaper, the **Pittsburgh Leader**, offered her a job as a drama critic, she left the magazine in favor of the newspaper.

Doubts began to assail her concerning the wisdom of continuing her present kind of activity. She wanted very much to write a book of fiction, but she was so busy with her newspaper work that she had neither the time nor the energy to begin such a project. She knew that it would take much time and effort to write a novel, and doubts assailed her about the probable success of such a venture. Finally she compromised by quitting the job that she held and taking a teaching position which left her with much more free time than she formerly had.

Now she began writing in earnest, both poetry and stories. Her first book of poems she called **April Twilights,** published in 1903 when she was 30 years old. It was not an outstanding success, but it gave her a new feeling of confidence. She had proved to herself that she could write well enough to have her work published, and that meant much to her. Now many short stories were written by her, one of which was published in the nationally known **McClure's Magazine.**

If such a famous magazine showed great enough interest in her work to publish one of her stories, perhaps it would accept others, she thought. Why, she actually had enough for a book! Why not send them to the editors of **McClure's Magazine** and ask that they be considered for collective publication in book form? The thought was father to the deed, and soon the manuscripts were on their way to the publishers.

At this point, a strange quirk of fate intervened. The short-story manuscripts were received and read by the editors, but they were rejected. However, before they were returned to Miss Cather they were by chance read by Mr. McClure himself, who was so impressed by them that he made a personal journey to Pittsburgh to see her. There he agreed to publish two of the stories in his magazine and the rest of them were to be printed in book form as she had so much desired. The book was a success and it added to her ever-increasing stature in the literary world. Equally as pleasing to her was the offer from **McClure's Magazine** to be an editor of that famous periodical.

Now began a new phase in her already interesting life, the following years being fascinating ones for her. She traveled much, even being sent to Europe by the publishing company. She made new and stimulating acquaintances and had ready access to the best homes. This kind of life pleased her and satisfied a deep longing for companionship that had its origin in the years that were spent in the lonely prairie country. The work was demanding and little time was found for any creative writing in the form of fiction, which, after all, was the kind that gave her the greatest satisfaction. She began to realize that the years were slipping by with nothing more accomplished than the mere fulfilling of her job requirements. Clearly, something had to be done.

What she decided to do took courage. It was not easy to give up a well-paying and respected literary position that brought her into contact with many of the outstanding people of her time. However, she had made up her mind that it must be done if she were to fulfill her natural destiny. She was approaching forty years of age and she knew that if she waited much longer, she would never be able to force herself to start life over again in a new career. In 1911 she gave up her position with the company that had done so much for her and began seriously to work on a novel.

A year later it was published. She called it **Alexander's Bridge,** and it was given encouraging recognition, but it was not signally successful, being about wealthy and aristocratic people. She realized that she must change her direction. She published another one, **O Pioneers!** the next year, to be followed by **Song of the Lark,** the central character being an opera singer. In 1918 **My Antonia** appeared, its setting in Nebraska and its characters the plain prairie people that she knew so well. This book has been called one of the best novels ever written by an American author. Four years later her **One of Ours** won the coveted Pulitzer prize in literature and her fame was assured. Other books were published, including the popular **Death Comes for the Archbishop,** its setting being in the desert country of southwestern United States. After **Lucy Gayheart** appeared in 1933, Willa Cather wrote only one more novel in the seventeen remaining years of her life. Entitled **Sapphira and the Slave Girl,** it had its setting in Virginia where she was born.

Willa Cather died in 1947 at the age of seventy-three. She had lived a full life, achieving recognition as one of America's great writers. Although born in obscurity and living in an isolated frontier community during her early years, through her own initiative and strength of character she realized the high goals that she set for herself.

Molly Pitcher

Heroine of the Battle of Monmouth

Many were the hardships that the people of this country went through during the years when General Washington and his brave men were fighting for freedom from our mother country, England. Sometimes the outlook was so black that few people believed that we could win our fight for liberty and independence. This was especially true during the hard winter of 1777 when Washington and his soldiers suffered through the cold months at Valley Forge, outside of Philadelphia. Ragged, cold and hungry, they were ill prepared to win battles against the seasoned British troops. However, their hearts were in the fight and they were determined to win. These two things almost made up for the many things that were lacking.

Spring came at last, and with it, renewed hope. The British general, Clinton, decided to take his army to New York, and Washington was just as determined to keep him out of that important city. The two armies met at Monmouth, in New Jersey, and a fierce battle took place.

In the thick of the fighting was a young Irishman named Tom. All day long he had stood by one of the cannons, firing shot after shot into the enemy's ranks. By his side was his brave wife, Molly, who had followed her husband to the war, going with him from camp to camp, always ready to do what she could to help. On this day at Monmouth she had gone many times to a nearby spring to bring water to the hot and thirsty soldiers. The heat of the summer took its toll among the tired and wounded men, but Molly never faltered in her efforts to make them more comfortable.

Molly was still but a girl, but she had already lived a very exciting life. She was born on a farm in New Jersey, and as soon as she was old enough to help her father, she was a willing worker, helping with the many chores that had to be done daily. She was a strong girl and often surprised her father by unusual feats of strength. She was a cheerful child with blue eyes and red hair, and she possessed an unfailing sense of optimism. If things weren't exactly as she wished them to be she did not grumble, but made the best of each situation.

When she was still fifteen years old she married a young man by the name of John Hayes. Today this would be regarded as a very young age for a girl to marry, but in those days many girls married when they were still in their early "teens," so no one was surprised when Molly became John's bride. At the time, Molly was working as a maid in the household of a Dr. Irvine of Philadelphia, and what was unusual was the fact that she continued in this capacity even after she was married.

Whether it was the lack of a real home that caused the rift in her domestic life or what it was, no one seemed to know, but as time went by Molly and John gradually drifted apart and eventually became separated, but not before Molly had had a taste of army life. Meanwhile, John had enlisted in the army as did many another man in those stirring times as fighting had broken out in Massachusetts and the revolution that was to separate the colonies from their mother country had begun. From ancient times it had been the custom for many of the wives of soldiers to follow their husbands as they went from place to place and from battle to battle. Molly now did this, joining John and following him as Washington's army moved from one place to another.

It was sometime during the hectic days of the early part of the war that Molly and John agreed to separate. Molly had met a young

Irish soldier with hair as red as her own, and quickly became attracted to him. After they were married they continued this kind of life together, never settling down in one place. Life was not easy for either of them. Often the army was on the move and they had to be ready to break camp at a moment's notice. Their home was a tent which became as ragged as their own clothes as the war dragged on, for supplies were few and unsatisfactory.

Congress then did not have the broad powers that it has today. In fact, all Congress could do was to ask each state to contribute to the common cause, but it had no way of enforcing its requests. The result was that many of the needs of the army were not met, and at times General Washington was so discouraged that he did not know how long he could continue the war. Food, clothing, ammunition, and other necessary items of war were usually very scarce and Molly and her husband were forced to endure many hardships. However, their faith in the cause for which they were fighting was strong and their love for General Washington was sincere, so they accepted their lot patiently and hoped for better days to come.

Molly never thought of herself as any kind of a hero. She was just a common soldier's wife with no thought of ever being anything else. Then fate decreed otherwise and Molly became a true hero of the Revolution. On many an evening around the campfires her name was sung in songs of praise for the heroic work that she did one day on a field of battle.

It was on the twenty-eighth of June in the year 1778 that fame came to Molly. It was Sunday and a terrible battle was taking place. The scene was at Monmouth, in New Jersey. The heat of the day was so great that many of the soldiers on both sides were overcome. Perhaps the ragged Colonial troops were better off than the British and their hired allies, the German Hessians, for few of them had regular uniforms. Instead, they dressed as best they could, and since it was summer, their clothing was light. The British, however, wore woolen uniforms and the Hessians not only wore heavy army attire, but they were loaded down with gear besides. All of the men on that day suffered greatly from the heat, the wounded men being in an especially pitiable condition.

During that day's battle, as on many others, Molly did everything that she could to help her husband and the other soldiers as well. One of her customary tasks was to carry water to them from some nearby source. At Monmouth a spring was found on the battlefield and Molly worked for many hours without stopping, carrying water from it to the men on the firing line. Water was needed not only to cool their perspiring faces and to quench their thirst, but to clean out the cannon, made dirty by constant firing.

"Molly, bring the pitcher!" they would call to her, and she would respond by taking cool water to them. Soon they were saying, "Molly, come with the pitcher!" or simply, "Molly, pitcher!"

The battle was not going well for the hot and tired Colonial troops. General Charles Lee, for some unaccountable reason, ordered a retreat, and had it not been for the timely intervention of General Washington, the day would have been a sad one of defeat for the American colonials. General Washington angrily censured Charles Lee for his misconduct, and the soldiers cheered his action.

During the height of the battle, Molly was dismayed to see her husband stagger and fall beside the cannon which he had been firing throughout the day. Other soldiers rushed up to take his place, but brave Molly was there before them. Quickly she rammed a charge into the cannon and fired it in the enemy's direction. Again and again she did this as the men about her cheered. Here was no ordinary woman, they agreed; this was Molly Pitcher, the heroine.

All through the long afternoon she manned the gun. Her husband had been carried away to be better cared for in a place of lesser danger and she would see him when the battle ended. Right now she had a soldier's work to do.

General Nathanael Greene, one of Washington's most trusted aides, came by and praised her bravery, then rode away to tell General Washington of the woman who was doing such valiant work on the field of battle.

The fighting ended when darkness mercifully descended on the field, but there was no rest for Molly. Leaving the cannon, she hurried away to find her wounded husband and to care for him through the night. In the morning, still barefooted with her face blackened by the stains of exploding powder, Molly was summoned to appear before General Washington. Gratefully he acknowledged her services and praised her for the work that she had done the day before. Lafayette was there, too, and he presented her with a gift of coins contributed by his officers.

It was a wonderful day for Molly Pitcher, not only for the honors which had come to her, but also because the thoughtful Washington gave her the rank of sergeant then and there, so that she could later qualify for a pension.

Molly was now a true part of the army and she remained a part of it through the remainder of the war and even after it ended. Her husband lived, but never fully recovered from the wounds that he received that day at Monmouth. After he died she left the army and returned to the less exciting life of a civilian.

As she grew older her health declined and she could no longer work to support herself as she once could. The Pennsylvania legislature then voted her a small pension which helped to ease the burdens of her old age. In 1832, over a half century after her memorable exploit at Monmouth, she died at the age of seventy-eight. On the 100th anniversary of our independence, on July 4, 1876, a monument was erected to her at Carlisle, Pennsylvania, where she is buried, dedicated to the "Heroine of Monmouth."

Molly Pitcher did not leave to the world great poems or the memory of cultural achievements accomplished, but she did leave an example of bravery that will survive as long as there is an America that is proud of its heroes and heroines. For her bravery at a time of crisis, Molly Pitcher will not be forgotten.

Susan B. Anthony

Champion of Women's Rights

It can truly be said of Susan Brownell Anthony that she changed the world. How one woman could do this makes a fascinating story.

Imagine if you can what America was like when she was a girl. We were a pioneer nation, growing rapidly, expanding westward, rich and becoming richer every year. All of this was good, for we were moving ever forward and in the right direction. But there was one very strange thing about this husky new country of ours—it was a **man's** country, decidedly and definitely. Women could not vote in elections, they could not hold public office, they could not even keep any money that they might earn if they had the opportunity to earn any, without their husband's consent. Even the poorest and least desirable kind of a man had rights far greater than any woman, no matter how brilliant or educated she might be, just because he was a man and she was a woman. And—oh, yes! Women could not attend college either. They were for men only, just as some of them are even to this day.

Don't think that most women were unhappy about their lot, for they were not. They accepted it as a fact, and that was that. Some of them, however, thought it was very unfair to women to deny them these rights and said so. Susan B. Anthony was one of them and she did more than anyone else to bring about a change.

Women's place was in the home, it was said then. Let the men run the world, as they had done since the dawn of history and even before that. Hadn't Adam been created first, and then Eve, as a sort of an afterthought, to serve man? That is the way it had been and that is the way it should stay, most people thought. But Susan Anthony did not think so and she determined to do something about it.

Susan was born on February 15 in the state of New York in the year 1820. Her parents were Quakers, and this fortunate circumstance had much to do in shaping Susan's philosophy and in determining her life's work. Her father was an intelligent and sensible man who encouraged his daughter during the many years that she spent in her efforts to secure equal rights for women, and at times helped her financially. He took a deep interest in the activities of his children, and the fact that all of them became prominent persons, active in social and political movements, is a tribute to his fatherly concern.

When Daniel Anthony moved with his family to Battenville, New York, he proceeded at once to establish a private school there which his children could attend, for he wanted to give his daughters a good education in spite of the fact that the colleges and universities of the day did not admit women as students. He also hired a tutor to give the girls private instruction in order to give them every advantage possible.

As a Quaker, Daniel Anthony did not believe in war nor in supporting a government that engaged in war. Yet he wanted to be a law-abiding citizen. At times these views presented real problems for him, but he always did what he thought was right and encouraged his children to do the same thing. His sons Daniel and Jacob went to faraway Kansas to fight the advancement of slavery in that territory, and Jacob became a member of John Brown's band which raided the town of Ossawatomie. John Brown was later hanged for his subsequent raid on Harper's Ferry.

The Quakers, or Society of Friends as they were called, regarded women as equal to the men in all religious matters, and Susan was still a young girl when she noticed this difference in their attitude. When Susan became a teacher after her father's business failed and he was declared bankrupt, she thought that it was not fair that she was receiving only two or three dollars a week for her services while the men teachers received several times that much. Also, she was appalled when she attended her first teacher's convention and became aware that although two out of every three of the delegates attending were women, all of the business was transacted by the men. No women spoke at any of the meetings simply because they were not permitted to do so. When she arose to speak her mind about this disturbing state of affairs, the chairman was very surprised and had to ask the delegates present to vote to approve permitting her to take part in the discussions.

When she was permitted to speak, she gave the men teachers something to really think about. She said, "In our country today women are not considered smart enough to become doctors or lawyers or preachers. However, they are thought to have brains enough to teach school. So every one of you men here today is admitting that he has no more brains than a woman." She had made her point well, so she sat down. Immediately the men voted to adjourn the meeting.

It was a small beginning, but it was a victory, and Susan was pleased about it, but she was dissatisfied with the opportunities that teaching offered her to work at her favorite reforms, women's rights and temperance. For fifteen years she had taught school in various places. During all of this time the conviction grew within her that she could be using her time to better advantage. She had joined the organization known as the Daughters of Temperance and found much satisfaction in the work that she was doing. Why not quit teaching and devote all of her time to professional reforming? It was a thrilling idea which she immediately wrote to her father about. To her great joy he not only approved of the idea, but offered to give her enough financial assistance to enable her to live without having to work to earn money, thereby making it possible to devote all of her time to the new project. At the age of thirty-three she entered upon this new phase of activity to which she was to devote the rest of her long life, for she lived to complete more than a half-century in this work that she loved so well.

Her plan was not only to speak and write to get her ideas before the public, but to form an organization which would have for its purpose the advancement of women's rights. She determined to travel throughout New York State, speaking to groups, going into homes, to get her message to both men and women. Then she planned to call a state convention which in turn would submit its demands to the state legislature. That lawmaking body would then be asked to make it legal for married women to own property in their own name, to have a right to their own earnings, to sue and be sued, and to vote. There were other objectives also, but these and the added one of making the mother as much of a guardian as the father over their minor children were the most important ones.

All through the long cold winter of 1853-1854, Susan and her helpers worked, traveling from one end of New York State to the other. Often they were ill-treated and insulted, by women as well as by men, for strangely enough many women were content with things as they were and had no interest in the women's rights movements. When the State Legislature met in Albany, a bill was introduced which proposed to give women the rights that they demanded. Ten thousand signatures on a petition backed up the sponsors of the bill, but it was doomed to failure right from the start. Overwhelmingly, it was voted down.

Susan B. Anthony was not a quitter. Anyone who worked as hard as she did and believed so wholeheartedly in what she was doing could not quit after only one defeat. At once she began again, preparing for the next session of the legislature. Again the fatiguing rounds began, with more meetings, more speeches, more home visits, more insults—and again defeat before the legislature. The next year's efforts were as futile, as were the next and the next one after that, but Susan never let up on these efforts. Seven times she took her cause to the legislature before that body approved the bill that she sponsored. At last it was the law of the state of New York, passed in the year 1860. Married women could now enter into contracts, could sue in their own names and be sued, and have the right to hold property and to have possession of their own earnings. Equally as important, they were now guardians, with their husbands, over their own children.

It was a great victory, gained after many years of toil, and to Susan B. Anthony belonged the credit for it. Without her untiring efforts there would have been no such law, very probably not even a bill to be introduced in the legislature. Great as the victory was, to her it was but a beginning. There was so much more to be done, for America was a large country with many states.

The Civil War began, and with it, a great personal loss, for her father died before the conflict ended. Susan now organized the Woman's National Loyal League, which called for freeing the slaves, supporting the cause of the Union, and the granting of women's rights. The right to vote was not yet theirs and that must be secured before there could be any rest for the militant crusader. When the war ended, the slaves had been freed and the Union saved, but there remained yet the securing of women's rights. She knew it would be a long and arduous fight, but she entered it willingly, for the rewards would be great.

Susan Anthony entered the campaign with her usual vigor. From one city to another she traveled, talking to large groups and small groups and to individuals. She was insulted, reviled, and subjected to indignities. Once acid was thrown at her, but none of it struck her face, though her clothing was burned. She was heckled at meetings and accosted on the streets. Drunken men made sport of her, and newspaper cartoons printed caricatures that depicted her indecently and immorally. Through it all she endured the slander with calmness and fortitude. Her cause was just and she knew it; nothing else mattered.

The objective of her crusade was to obtain the passage of a Constitutional amendment which would give women the right to vote. The Fourteenth Amendment already defined a citizen as anyone who was born in the United States or who had become an American citizen through naturalization. "Anyone" certainly included women!

To test out her theory, Susan Anthony demanded that she be permitted to cast her ballot in an election, but was afterward arrested for the "crime" of voting illegally and was fined $100.00. She never paid the fine, though she was jailed for a short period of time.

Though she had been active in her campaigns for over a half-century, she refused to quit. She reached the age of eighty before she stepped down as president of the organization that had done so much to advance the cause that she sponsored, but she nevertheless remained active in the work of the group.

In the early spring of the year 1906 she went to Washington, D. C., to attend a meeting honoring her on her eighty-sixth birthday. There she gave her last public address. Tired out from the trip, she became ill upon returning to her home in Rochester, New York, and died within a few days. At last her work was ended, but the cause to which she had devoted her long life continued to gather strength. In 1920 the Nineteenth Amendment to the Constitution of the United States was adopted, giving women the right to vote.

Susan B. Anthony did not live to see the passage of this amendment, but she knew before she died that it was but a matter of time before it would become a part of our Constitution. She was happy in this knowledge, for it was her handiwork, a long, long labor of love.

Sacajawea

The Bird Woman

About the time our forefathers were establishing a new and different kind of government for the infant United States of America, a baby girl was born in a tribe of Indians living in the far Western lands. As was customary among these Shoshone Indians, she was given a name that was made up at the time of birth, often related to some unusual sight, even to an animal that came to the parents' attention at the moment. That is why we can recall today such names as Crazy Horse, Sitting Bull, Little Crow, Flying Cloud, and others of similar kind.

Why the baby was called Sacajawea, or "Bird Woman," is not known, but almost certainly a bird of some kind must have made its appearance about the tepee when she was born, and so, according to custom, this was regarded as significant enough to give the little baby its name. As she grew older, the appropriateness of her name became more and more apparent. She was as alert and observant as a wild bird, and as cheerful. She sang as she went about her work, and her actions were always kindly and never harmful.

One day a terrible thing happened to Sacajawea. She was still a small child when the Shoshone village was raided by an enemy tribe of Hidatsa Indians and she was carried off by them as they fled after the sudden attack. Her father was the chief of the Shoshones, but even he failed to rescue her. She was taken far to the east, over five hundred miles away from her parents and playmates. There she grew to young womanhood.

Living with the Hidatsa tribe was a French Canadian by the name of Charbonneau. Sacajawea was such a pretty child, as small and cheerful as a prairie sparrow, and Charbonneau was attracted to her. It was customary in those days for Indians to sell their captives if they could, usually for a good pony, or sometimes even two. It is not known what price had to be paid for her, but a deal was made and Sacajawea became the property of Charbonneau. When she was fourteen years old, a marriage ceremony was held and the two were married. It was not the kind of wedding that is held today, but one in agreement with the custom of the tribe. It must be remembered that all of this happened a long time ago, before the customs of civilized people were even heard of in that faraway Rocky Mountain region.

So Sacajawea became the bride of a Canadian adventurer and explorer and went "housekeeping" in a brand-new tepee that was set up for them, as was done for all newlywed couples. Several years went by and Sacajawea had little hope of ever returning to her own people far to the west. When she was seventeen years old, a baby was born to her, and now she felt that life was complete. Little did she know that soon she was to begin an adventure that would give her far more happiness than she had ever known.

The Hidatsa tribe was living in the Missouri River territory, for it was there that the buffalo came to feed and to drink. It was from these huge shaggy beasts that the Indians received not only food, but clothing and shelter as well, as the animals' skins were large and tough. One day a party of white men came up the river and stopped at the Hidatsa village. They had horses along with them, and their home was a big barge that was pulled along by ropes. It was the first such group of white men that had ever come into that region and the Indians were greatly excited by their coming.

Who were these white men who were now so far from their homes, in a strange and wild land inhabited only by savage Indians?

They were the members of the famed Lewis and Clark expedition, sent by President Thomas Jefferson to explore the vast Louisiana Territory recently purchased from France. The year was 1805 and Sacajawea was seventeen years old. Her baby had been born just two months before this.

Charbonneau, her husband, agreed to serve as guide for the party of white men, and Sacajawea eagerly agreed to go with him. It would mean that they would pass through the country of the Shoshones and that she would once more see her own people. Strapping her tiny baby on her back, she set out at once with the exploring party, prepared to endure all of the hardships of the trail, for she knew that there would be many of them.

Although it was unusual for a woman to be taken along on such a journey, her presence proved to be of real value to the white men. She was intelligent and reliable, making herself constantly useful in many ways. She was wise in the ways of the prairie Indians and was able to cure many a man's illness through the use of roots and herbs. The expedition had no doctor, relying upon Captain Lewis' medicine box for remedies. But usually the Indian maid's potions were more effective than the white man's medicines.

One day Sacajawea recognized a landmark. At last they were coming into Shoshone country! She had long been eagerly searching the horizon for familiar land features and now she saw her first one. Lewis and Clark were glad that she was along with them for it meant that they would receive a friendly reception from the Shoshones, through whose territory they would have to pass.

When the moment came when she was united with her people, it was a touching scene. Indians seldom showed their emotions, but the occasion was too much for Sacajawea who had looked forward for such a long time to the reunion. She wept openly and was not ashamed, but they were tears of joy. The Shoshones were amazed at her return and welcomed the white men to their country.

Sacajawea's true character was shown a few days later when she learned that the Shoshones, under the leadership of her brother, were plotting to steal the expedition's horses. If the plan had been successful it would probably have meant the end of the expedition, for it could not have gone on without its horses. However, Sacajawea's loyalty to her white friends was too great to permit this to happen and she told the leaders about the plot. More than ever the men now realized the true worth of the little Bird Woman who had been endearing herself to them through the long weeks of the journey.

On another occasion, this remarkable young woman saved the valuable records of the expedition when a canoe tipped over. Acting instantly, at the risk of her life, with her baby strapped to her back, she leaped into the river and rescued the records before they were washed away. Captain Lewis said afterward that the loss would have been virtually irreplaceable and would probably have resulted in a year's delay for the expedition.

They went on up the Missouri River and across the Rocky Mountains until their objective, the Pacific Ocean, was reached. Then they began their long journey back toward their homes. It was spring of the next year before they reached Sacajawea's home territory again, there to separate from the expedition. It is said that Charbonneau was paid handsomely for his services, but that the loyal and useful Sacajawea received no money, for she was merely the wife of the expedition's guide! However, Captain Clark was profuse in his praise of her and wrote in the official journal a glowing account of her services to the expedition.

Their parting was a sad one, for the men had become very fond of little Baptiste Charbonneau and his parents. Captain Clark told the couple that if they came to St. Louis he would help them to get a start in farming near that city. Three years after they parted, Sacajawea and her husband and son went to St. Louis where they did engage in farming for some time, but they missed their home country and soon returned to the broad plains of the Missouri.

In the summer of 1812, Sacajawea gave birth to her second child, a girl. Four months later she died at the age of twenty-five years.

Her death was recorded in the records of the fort where she had been living, the clerk adding the words, "She was a fine woman, the best in the fort."

Her life was a short one, but it had been packed with experiences such as no other woman of the time had been privileged to enjoy. Everywhere she went, she became a favorite because of her sunny disposition and likeable ways.

Captain Clark spoke for all who knew her when he wrote in his journal, "Intelligent, cheerful, resourceful, tireless, faithful, she inspired us all."

Martha Washington

America's First Lady

The wife of the "Father of Our Country" was a person who was so overshadowed by her illustrious husband that few people came to know her well during her lifetime. Fewer still today are familiar with the details of her life, though she was not only an interesting person, but one who lived a full and satisfying life. The fact that she was a very modest woman who was content to be simply the wife of George Washington and never sought the limelight or tried in any way to project herself into public affairs makes her comparatively little-known life history all the more interesting.

Martha Dandridge was born in 1732, the same year as her husband, near the beautiful colonial city of Williamsburg in Virginia. Her father, Colonel John Dandridge, owned a plantation nearby and by standards of those times was a wealthy man. Their home was near the site of Jamestown where Captain John Smith had, in the previous century, begun the first English colony in America. It was also near the village of Yorktown, later made famous when General Washington captured the British General Cornwallis there and so ended the Revolutionary War which made the colonies a free and independent nation.

Martha's girlhood was typical of that of other girls of that day who lived in similar circumstances. She did not attend a country school, for plantations such as the one on which she lived were large and there were not enough children living within the area to warrant maintaining a public school. She was taught in her own home, her schooling consisting of the usual three R's of that time: reading, 'riting, and 'rithmetic.

More important than the fundamentals of reading and spelling were the social graces: learning how to act properly, to dress well, and to eat with good manners. Girls of good parentage expected to marry well and to have their own homes some day, so it was regarded as highly important to teach them the best manners. Martha learned all of these things well, so when she grew to womanhood and, as George Washington's wife, became mistress of Mount Vernon, she added grace and charm to the lovely home.

Martha, like so many girls of colonial days, married very young. Her husband was not quite twice her age of seventeen, but almost. He, too, was a plantation owner, so the two of them felt that they had married well and within their stations in life. Daniel Custis, her husband, was frail and not at all blessed with good health, and their children were like their father in that respect. Two children were born to them and both died in infancy. Then a son was born who lived, but was frail, and later, just as the father died, a daughter arrived. Martha Custis was still young and attractive and now she was a widow who possessed much land and wealth. In fact, she was regarded as one of the wealthiest women in the colonies.

It was about a year later that by chance George Washington, journeying on horseback to Williamsburg on official government business, met the charming young widow. There was an immediate and mutual attraction between the two. He was twenty-six, wealthy in his own right, tall and imposing in his uniform and prominent in the affairs of the Virginia colony. She was of the same age, attractive, wealthy, and lonely. George Washington returned to Martha's home only a week or so later and before he left he had asked for her hand in marriage. She demurred, as good manners decreed that she should, but there unquestionably was an agreement between them following this second meeting that culminated in their marriage on the sixth day of the new year, 1759. Both bride and groom were twenty-seven years of age. They settled down at Mount Vernon, which George Washington had inherited upon the death of his half-brother, Lawrence. It was a magnificent estate located on the banks of the Potomac, with the mansion set high on a hill overlooking the broad river.

The years following their marriage were happy ones. They had no children of their own, but Washington adored Martha's two little ones and always looked upon them as his own. When his foster daughter sickened and died when she was still in her teens, Washington was heartbroken and grieved greatly over the loss of the young lady whom he loved dearly. Jack Custis, Martha's son, lived with her at Mount Vernon until he married and left to make a home of his own.

War clouds were lowering over the colonies, and in 1775 the fighting began in faraway Massachusetts. At Lexington and Concord, near Boston, the first clashes occurred, followed by the terrible battle of Bunker Hill, across the Charles River from Boston. Now a man was needed to be the commander-in-chief of the raw colonial troops who could lead them to victory over the well-trained British regulars. There was general agreement that this man should be none other than George Washington who had saved the remnants of Braddock's army after it was ambushed by the French and Indians near Fort Duquesne and who was perhaps the colonies' outstanding military man.

When the call came to serve his country as commander-in-chief, George Washington responded with a will, but nevertheless sadly. Now he would have to be away from his beloved Mount Vernon, perhaps never to return. If he should be captured by the British he would surely be hanged. If the colonies' attempt at independence should fail, he would lose everything that he had in the world, including Mount Vernon. As long as the war was in progress he would be in danger of death either by shellfire or disease, both of which exacted a heavy toll among the soldiers.

In spite of these bleak possibilities, Martha Washington knew that her husband could give no other answer but the one that he did. She knew that the home would be lonely without him, but she knew, too, that the call to duty could not be resisted. Sadly she watched him ride away, for how long, she knew not. His destination was Cambridge, near Boston, and it was there that he took command of the troops that he was to lead for so many years.

No sooner was he gone than Martha began to plan to join him. It was now summer, but winter would soon follow, when fighting would cease during the cold months. Then the army would go into winter quarters and Martha would journey north to spend the winter at headquarters with her husband. It was November when she set out on the long journey, accompanied by her son. She rode in her own horse-drawn coach over hundreds of miles of roads that were narrow and rough, with only crude accommodations awaiting her at the end of the day.

The miles were long and weary ones from Virginia to Massachusetts, and the Christmas season had arrived before the journey ended. Now they could spend a few months together again before the General once more had to begin the summer campaign that kept his army moving for many months. Martha then looked to the southward and began the long return journey to Mount Vernon in Virginia.

Year after year during the long war Martha Washington rode to be with her husband during the winter months wherever the army might be. During several of these winters, such as those at Morristown and Valley Forge, the suffering of the soldiers was great. Ill-clad, poorly fed, and unpaid, many deserted, until by spring there was but a skeleton of an army left. Then it was that Martha Washington showed her true mettle. Though an aristocrat in every sense of the word, she knit mittens and socks for the suffering men, and darned the socks of those who wore holes in them while drilling or on guard duty. She patched their coats and sewed on buttons and all of the men praised her for her devotion to them.

Three more years went by. Cornwallis took up his quarters at Yorktown and quickly Washington decided that the time had come for a decisive blow to be dealt which might well end the war. He hurried south, but no one knew his destination. For the first time in six years he saw Mount Vernon, stopping only momentarily to take their son Jack along with him as an aide. Then he hurried on, to bottle up Cornwallis at Yorktown. Resistance was futile, for the French fleet shut off both help and escape by sea and Washington's men prevented escape by land. Cornwallis surrendered, but Jack, frail and ill, died during the campaign. Martha had now lost all of her four children.

Two more years went by before peace was declared, but during this time Martha was with her husband at all times. Now she had no one but him to turn to for consolation. With the return of peace they both gratefully returned home, with only one thought, that never again would they be separated. But fate decreed otherwise, for with the adoption of the new Constitution, the call to service came to him once more, this time to take up his duties in the highest post to which his people could elevate him, that of President of the United States. Reluctantly he again departed from Mount Vernon, but now Martha went with him, to serve as First Lady of America. This she did with grace and distinction for eight years. The honor of the position was great, but the responsibilities were heavy for both of them.

In 1797 his second term of office ended and Martha and her husband returned to Mount Vernon, longing for the quiet life of the plantation. There for two years their dream was realized, for though the children were gone, they had each other and that was all that mattered. One December day in the year 1799, George Washington rode over his broad acres for the last time, for the day was wet and cold and he caught a severe chill from which he died.

Martha was now truly alone. She never knew how lonesome life could be without the man with whom she had shared so many years of her life. For three years she continued to live in the family home overlooking the Potomac River, then she, too, succumbed to a fever.

The tomb of George and Martha Washington stands just below the Mount Vernon mansion. Thousands of Americans visit it every year, for it is to them a sacred shrine. In reverence they stand before the tomb in which lie the mortal remains of George Washington, father of his country, and of his beloved wife Martha, who, with him, holds a hallowed spot in the hearts of all Americans.

Elizabeth Palmer Peabody

Friend of the Kindergarten

Almost all children who have ever attended a kindergarten look back upon those early days of their schooling as a time of pleasure and happiness. The man who established the first kindergarten school intended it to be such a place, where children would like to come to play, to be with friends, and to learn from a kindly teacher. His name was Frederick Froebel, and since he lived in Germany, he gave his new school a German name. He called it a kindergarten, which meant a "children's garden." When people of this country spoke of Froebel's school, they, too, referred to it as a kindergarten, keeping the German name, and so it is known today, over a hundred years after the first English-speaking kindergarten was opened in the United States.

The person who began this school lived in Boston and she belonged to a well-known family of that cultured city. Her name was Elizabeth Peabody and she was born in the year 1804, when Thomas Jefferson was President of the United States and there were few people living west of the Eastern row of states, for our country had won its independence from England less than thirty years before. Her father was a dentist whose earnings were so small that his wife had to earn money to help support the family. When his daughters grew up they, too, became wage earners, teaching school to make a living. The Peabody family, however, had long been prominent in

Massachusetts and they counted many of the important people of the state to be among their best friends. Both of Elizabeth's sisters married men who became famous, Mary becoming Mrs. Horace Mann, a prominent educator, and Sophia marrying Nathaniel Hawthorne, one of America's greatest authors.

Although Elizabeth had several proposals of marriage, she remained single all her life. She was too busy to give time to household duties, she said. So when men sought her out and gave her their attention, she was careful not to encourage them. She once said that when she felt that the time had come for her to marry, she could certainly do so, but evidently that time never came, in her opinion.

Her mother had begun a school in the home when Elizabeth was still small, so when Elizabeth grew old enough to help her mother, she became a very busy teen-ager. She sometimes sighed a bit because she was unable to spend more time at play with neighborhood children, but she enjoyed her teaching duties and was glad to help her mother in this way.

Because she began early to assist with her mother's work, it was natural that she would become a teacher in her own right when she became older, and this is what happened. At that time the family lived in Salem, an historic old town on the coast just above Boston. She had received years of instruction at home and had become an excellent Latin student under the tutelage of her father who had once been a Latin teacher in a famous academy. Now, at the age of eighteen, she decided to learn Greek also. She left her Salem home to go to nearby Boston where she opened a school of her own. She became acquainted with a young minister named Ralph Waldo Emerson who helped her with her Greek lessons. Little did she know then that he was to become one of America's best-known citizens in later years, but the two of them remained good friends throughout their lives.

Elizabeth had never been more than a few miles from home, so when the opportunity came for her to become a governess in a family that lived in Maine, she gladly accepted, and took a steamship up the coast. Her employer was a doctor who had a large library in his home which Elizabeth was permitted to use, much to her delight. There were books written in French and Latin and Greek, all of which she could read proficiently. She joined a young people's study club and for a time almost thought of herself as being in love with one of the young men members, but when he asked her to marry him, she refused. She was not ready to "settle down to housekeeping," as she expressed it. There were too many things to do yet, she declared.

Restless, she gave up her position in Maine and moved to Brookline near Boston where she opened a day school. She was a very popular teacher, but not a good manager, and before long she was forced to close the school because of financial reasons.

She now turned to writing as a career and wrote a series of history books which were published. However, they did not earn much money for her so she became a lecturer. She was the only woman lecturer thereabouts and many people considered it to be quite a daring thing for her to do. She liked her new work very much and was regarded as a successful lecturer, but once more she quit that work to return to teaching.

Another prominent family in Massachusetts was the Alcott family, and when Elizabeth Peabody heard that Bronson Alcott was about to open a new school she at once offered to assist him. He accepted gladly, for she was regarded as an excellent teacher, but the school failed because of Alcott's unusual methods of teaching, and once again Elizabeth was out of a job.

Now she decided to open a book shop, though there were no women shopkeepers in Boston at that time and the very idea of one shocked many people. However, this short phase of her life proved to be an important one for it was because of her unusual vocation that she became acquainted with Froebel's kindergarten plan. In a way, it was a successful business venture, too, for many people of prominence came to examine her offerings. The famous philosopher, minister, and lecturer, Ralph Waldo Emerson, not only encouraged her, but came often to her shop. So did Henry Thoreau, one of our nation's great men and author of "Walden," the story of his lone stay in a little cabin on the shore of Walden Pond near Concord, and James Russell Lowell, the poet.

Elizabeth expanded her interests by setting up a printing shop in the bookstore and began publishing various literary offerings. An antislavery pamphlet was followed by Nathaniel Hawthorne's "Twice Told Tales." A magazine of essays and poems contributed by various authors also came from her little press. However, her income from this source was small, although she found the work stimulating and exciting.

While browsing among her books, Elizabeth noted with interest some of the writings of Frederick Froebel and his new kind of school that was called a kindergarten. Everything that he wrote, she agreed with. Children should be happy in school, he wrote, and it was important that they have pleasant experiences in play. They should learn to sing and to express themselves in music. They should learn about nature and art, all in a happy environment.

Now Elizabeth Peabody determined to bring this new kind of school to America. She would start her own kindergarten. Of course, she had no money, but that could be remedied—she would ask her friends to finance it! She had many wealthy friends who she was sure would help her to get started. She went to other educators to ask their opinions. She called on friends and acquaintances and asked them for funds.

Soon there was enough money pledged to enable her to begin her project. Hers was the first English-speaking kindergarten in America, though a woman in Milwaukee had begun one there several years earlier in which the children spoke German, for their parents had recently immigrated to America from Germany.

The people of Boston and vicinity were very pleased with the new school and Elizabeth Peabody quickly found herself to be quite a famous person. Now she decided that she must go to Germany to see for herself the kindergartens of that country just as Frederick

Froebel himself believed that they should be. The only deterring factor was that she did not have any money to pay for the trip. Again her many friends came to her rescue and soon over a thousand dollars had been raised to finance the trip. Elizabeth was thrilled not only by the money, but by the generosity of her friends.

The trip to Europe was everything that she had hoped for and more. She visited not only kindergartens, but cathedrals, museums, universities, and galleries in which the world's greatest art objects were on display. In the German kindergartens every detail was carefully noted, for she wanted her American counterpart to be as much like the German original as possible.

She hurried back to America and at once began to lecture on every possible occasion to encourage an interest in kindergartens. Nor did she limit her efforts to the vicinity of Boston, for soon kindergartens were being established in such cities as New York and in the faraway frontier town of St. Louis. Even California on the Pacific Coast heard of the new kind of school and soon one was opened in San Francisco. The founding of these schools was not enough, for well-trained teachers were needed if the kindergartens were to be successful. One such teacher-training school was begun in Boston and Elizabeth Peabody never ceased recruiting young women for the courses offered there.

The years went by, but Elizabeth Peabody never stopped her efforts on behalf of the children of America. She lived a long life, almost spanning the entire nineteenth century. Before she died in 1894 she had seen the kindergarten become a part of thousands of schools from one end of America to the other. Her greatest source of satisfaction lay in the knowledge that she had brought happiness into the lives of so many children. Today that happiness continues, for the kindergarten is now a recognized part of almost every American school system.

Emily Dickinson

Mystic and Poet

One of America's best-loved poets is Emily Dickinson, who lived during the nineteenth century. A frail little person, shy and retiring, she found the big world and its problems too much for her to cope with and so she withdrew from them, to live apparently content in a small world of her own creation. Her world was one of poetry and make-believe, gentle and kindly, so much different from the real world about her which she feared.

Emily was born in Massachusetts in the year 1830, when our nation of America was young and vigorously growing. Perhaps that is why she found it such a confusing, even frightening place in which to live. There was so much going on in the world about her, but her own home was so quiet and peaceful that she preferred it to the noisome and distracting world that surrounded her. Only once in her life did she leave Massachusetts, an experience that she seemed to enjoy very much, but which she never repeated. However, she wrote as if she were a seasoned traveler and drew upon her vivid imagination to supply the details that lack of actual experience had denied her. In one poem she wrote:

> "I never saw a moor,
> I never saw the sea;
> Yet know I how the heather looks,
> And what a wave must be."

In her home town of Amhurst, Edward Dickinson, Emily's father, was a well-known and highly respected man. He was a person of ability who through the years became wealthy through hard work and unswerving perseverance. His personality was stern to the point of harshness, with little sentiment in evidence. In his home he was domineering and in every sense of the term, "master of the house." How much the character of the father influenced the personality of his daughter Emily it is hard to say, but almost certainly her own individuality was suppressed by that of her dominant father. There never was a thought of anything but respect shown for him by members of his family, though love itself may well have been absent. A man with his traits of character would very probably have been much easier to respect than to love.

Emily's mother was almost the opposite kind of person. She was quiet, unassertive, and submissive to the will of her husband. Emily herself seemed to regard her mother as a rather ordinary type of person who apparently exerted very little influence in shaping the character and personality of her daughter.

There was nothing unusual about Emily's childhood years, one way or another. She and her younger sister Lavinia and her older brother Austin were much like other children of that time, taking part in their normal activities. However, there was a moodiness and an element of mysticism about Emily that at times came noticeably to the surface, this trait becoming more pronounced as she grew older.

Perhaps the sensitive girl was influenced by the unusual location of the family home, which stood directly across the street from the village cemetery. It was customary then, as it is in many localities today, for the funeral procession to go from the church where the services were held to the place of burial. On each occasion the long line of horse-drawn vehicles filed slowly down the street in front of the Dickinson home and into the cemetery entrance. At the head of the procession, conspicuous in its black drapery, was the hearse which contained the body of the deceased person. It was only natural that viewing this sight on so many occasions made a deep impression on Emily and was at least, to some extent, responsible for the melancholy view with which she grew to regard life itself.

When she was sixteen years old, Emily was sent away to school. That she missed her home and family very much was evident from the many letters which she wrote to them. She seemed happy in her new environment, but admittedly she was often homesick. She took part in many of the activities that the other girls of the school engaged in and seemingly was as fun-loving as any of them. When she returned home after an absence of a year she once more became interested in the routine affairs of the family, though her letters show that she missed the presence of Austin who was now away attending law school.

For several years her life continued in this fashion, with nothing to indicate that she would someday be regarded as her country's greatest poet. Certainly those who were closest to her never remarked about any noticeably outstanding characteristics. If anything, there was a monotony about the days which so quickly grew into years that one wonders just when the changes which occurred, both in her personality and in her creative ability, began to make themselves felt.

The one trip that was taken out of her native state was made to our national capital and it proved to be a thrilling experience. Accompanying her was Lavinia, her younger sister. Her father had been elected to serve his district as a member of the House of Representatives and both sisters were proud of the prominent position to which he had risen. On their way home they stopped off in Philadelphia to visit the historical buildings in that city and also to renew acquaintances with Helen Hunt, a friend of childhood days.

It was not long after this trip, when Emily was twenty-three years old, that a strange change began to take place in her personality, one that deeply affected her behavior and eventually altered her entire life. What brought this change about no one knows, though many persons have sought to find some clue that would explain it, but there are as many explanations as there are persons giving them. A tendency toward shyness increased little by little. She began to find excuses for not going with the other members of the family to church or she would stay at home when they went to visit friends. Sometimes when friends called at the home she would stay in her room in order not to see them or visit with them. The change was not a sudden one that attracted her family's attention nor was it at first alarming.

Such unusual behavior naturally caused comment, and her friends offered many suggestions, but the very fact that so many have been advanced suggests that they are speculations rather than true reasons. Many of the conjectures give an unhappy love affair as the reason for the change in Emily's personality and life pattern, but there is little evidence to support this suggestion. Emily herself never offered an explanation and her family did not suggest one.

At the age of twenty-three Emily had traveled to Washington and Philadelphia. At thirty-three she was a recluse, remaining within the protective walls of her home, not even willing to visit with those friends who called on her, preferring to talk to them from an adjoining room. She dressed only in white, causing a friend to remark, "How fortunate that she dresses in white! How terrible it would have been if she had chosen black!"

In her lonely life she sought emotional release in the writing of poetry, turning out hundreds of poems in the course of one year's time. Most of these poems were written during the earlier years of her seclusion, the number becoming smaller with the passing of time. She did not appear to be anxious about having them published, although she did submit them to critics for evaluation. Even the "experts," however, failed to recognize the rare genius of her poetry and did little to encourage her in her efforts.

One or two of her poems were published, but without attracting any special comment or attention. When an editor on his own behalf changed the wording of a poem that she submitted for publication she was both hurt and angry, causing a resentment to build up within her against editors in general.

It is probable that publishers showed little enthusiasm for her poems because they were different from the kind that was in vogue at that time. Not all of the lines rhymed, and in other ways they failed to conform to the pattern generally favored in that era. The meaning of life was reflected time and again in the delicate little poems that she composed in the seclusion of her room, and death, too, was an ever-fascinating subject.

When Emily was forty-four years old her father died. He had always accepted her as she was and never seemed to question the reasons for the strange change that had occurred in her way of life. The home was never the same afterward, and now Emily withdrew completely from the world and those who lived in it. They missed the stern and unyielding man who had so dominated the home but who had been so respected and admired by them all. During the years that elapsed between the death of the father and that of the daughter, never could the grieving Emily bring herself to visit his grave.

Another year went by and then the mother became an invalid. Emily and Lavinia took care of her in the big house where they had lived so long, but which was now changed from the carefree days of childhood. Fewer and fewer poems were written now. When the mother died of a heart ailment, Emily's life was more empty than ever. Death robbed her of both relatives and friends, and on each of death's visits she was left more disconsolate than ever. Then Emily, too, became ill and on a May morning in 1886 she died at the age of fifty-five.

Among her possessions were found many hundreds of poems. With care Lavinia went through them all, determined to have them published in memory of her sister. No one could she find who would do this, until one publisher agreed to put them in book form only if she would pay the publication costs. Sorrowfully she agreed, for she wanted Emily's poems to survive.

Before Lavinia died she had the satisfaction of knowing that her sister's poems were at last receiving recognition from the world at large. Many people were acclaiming her as America's greatest poet. Her only regret was that Emily was not there to receive these honors in person, but then she wondered if her mystic sister would have cared. Writing them had been her labor of love. Perhaps that was all that mattered.

Clara Barton

Founder of the American Red Cross

When disaster strikes, Red Cross representatives are the first ones there to give aid to the stricken. It may be a tornado in Kansas or a brush fire in California, an earthquake in Alaska or a flood somewhere in the Mississippi Valley, but wherever it happens, the Red Cross workers are there almost immediately with help. Sometimes it is an individual family that is stricken by fire or wind or accident and help is needed by them alone. Again, the Red Cross is there with help.

Millions of American people join the Red Cross each year, contributing money to that organization for the purpose of helping others. More millions of children, usually through their schools, are members of the Junior Red Cross and their pennies and nickels and dimes add up to an impressive total, all of which is used to help others in need. Many schools have Junior Red Cross units which contribute valuable materials such as bandages and clothing to the organization. In this way the children are taught early in life the value of service to others.

All of this worthy work was begun by a slight little lady only five feet tall, but who had an abundance of energy with which to put her ambitious plans into action. Her name was Clara Barton and she was the founder of the American Red Cross.

Clara Barton was born on a farm in Massachusetts in 1821 and lived the first years of her life there. Her father had been a soldier and an Indian fighter, and it was probably from him that Clara inherited much of her energy and ambition. She had two brothers and two sisters. The members of the family were always willing to help one another, and it was from her brothers and sisters that she first learned to read and to write. School facilities were not the best in rural areas in those days, but Clara was eager to learn and liked to go to school.

When Clara finished grade school she was offered a job as a teacher in the little country school that she had attended. So it came about that at the age of fifteen she was already instructing other children in the three R's. Some of the pupils of the school were boys who were bigger and older than she was, but usually she had no trouble making them behave, for the simple reason that they liked her. She was small but strong-willed, and when she determined to make a success of anything, that success was generally assured.

She was only eleven years old when one of her brothers fell from a barn roof during its construction, and for two years he was an invalid, requiring almost constant care. Clara took it upon herself to be his nurse, and so capable was she that the doctor attending her brother gave her complete charge since she showed herself to be so reliable. Eventually her brother recovered, but the two years that it took were given almost entirely to his care. At this early age she was already demonstrating the philosophy of service to others that guided her actions throughout her life.

The Barton family left Massachusetts and moved to Bordentown in New Jersey. The only school in town was a tuition school; that is, unless a tuition fee was paid, a child could not attend. Because of this, many children were receiving no schooling at all since their parents could not afford to pay the required fee. Clara Barton decided to do something about this deplorable condition.

What she did was to start a school of her own which would cost the pupils nothing. She was given the use of a large vacant building and there she began teaching, with six children enrolled. The news spread throughout the town that a wonderful young lady had opened a free school, and within a matter of weeks hundreds of children were flocking to Clara Barton's Bordentown school. The strain proved to be too much for her frail body and a breakdown followed, forcing her to give up the project which she had begun with such high hopes.

After she had recovered her strength, she looked about her for another position, one that would not tax her strength so greatly. Washington, our capital city, was an interesting place where there was much activity and she decided to go there, having received an offer of a job in the patent office. She liked the work, and as always, she did it well. For several years she continued in this position, and then the Civil War broke out.

It was a strange situation that our government faced. The war was between the states of the North and the states of the South, yet our national capital was actually in a Southern state! Sentiment in Maryland was strongly pro-Southern, and when soldiers from Clara's home state of Massachusetts were sent to defend Washington, they had to fight their way through the city of Baltimore. Many of them were injured in the rioting and when they arrived in Washington they were a pathetic group, even having lost their own personal possessions in the fight. Washington was not prepared for war and there were no supplies there to give to the soldiers.

With her usual concern for others, Clara decided to do something about the unfortunate situation. She inserted a paid notice in a Massachusetts newspaper asking for clothing and supplies for the discouraged men, many of whom were sick or wounded. The people of Massachusetts, appalled by the actions of the Maryland people and by the inadequacy of our national government to meet the emergency, responded both quickly and generously to her appeal. Now there was only one thing to do and that was to open an office in Washington to distribute the gifts received. This she did and soon she had an efficient agency operating, greatly impressing the government's officials.

Wounded soldiers began to arrive from the front lines, and Clara Barton was horrified by the manner in which many of them were permitted to die because of lack of attention. She was granted permission by the Surgeon General to do what she could for the unfortunate men who would otherwise have been given little, if any, attention. The number of army doctors was small and after a battle there were so many wounded men that the needs of very few of them could be met. There was only one solution, pleaded Clara, and that was to secure the help of many nurses. After every battle she worked herself to the point of exhaustion. During one of the bloodiest battles of the war, at Antietam, a bullet killed a soldier whom she was attending and another shot pierced her clothes. She seemed to live a charmed life, for on many battlefields she was exposed for hours to heavy shot and shell, yet she escaped injury and death. She became known as the Angel of the Battlefield, so bravely was her work done.

Everything that was needed to be done she did. Her first duty was to the wounded and to them she brought cooling water to drink and hot gruel to eat, which she often cooked herself. She washed and dressed their wounds and made them as comfortable as possible. All through the tragic years of the war she worked, mindless of herself, thinking only of others. When the war ended she spent four more years locating missing men whose families did not know their fates. Most of them were dead, victims of the war, but it was a consolation to the families to know where their sons and brothers were buried. Congress reimbursed her for the expenses that she had incurred, but not one cent of compensation did she get for the four years of hard work that she had put in tracing over 30,000 missing men.

Once again she suffered a breakdown due to the intense work of the past four years and she went to Switzerland to regain her strength. There she learned of the International Red Cross, for its headquarters were in Geneva, Switzerland. Its flag was a red cross on a white field, the reverse of the Swiss flag which was a white cross on a red field. The Franco-Prussian war broke out and Clara Barton at once went back to her work of aiding the sick and the wounded. She received many tributes and awards for her heroic efforts. In England Queen Victoria honored her by personally presenting her with an award. The war efforts proved to be too heavy a burden, for again her health broke and many more months were spent recuperating.

When she returned to America she began a long campaign to have this country become a part of the International Red Cross organization. This occurred in 1882 when Congress, by official action, made her President of the American Red Cross. Her services were in constant demand and she traveled much, always praising the work of the organization and advancing its cause.

In 1896, at the age of seventy-five, she went to faroff Turkey to help the sick and the wounded in a war that was then in progress. The Spanish-American War broke out and she returned to America to serve on the battlefields of Cuba. The city of Galveston, Texas, was devastated when the waters of the Gulf of Mexico flooded the city during a terrible storm and she hurried there to direct the rescue work, although almost eighty years of age.

Her age and the frail health that had been hers for so many years made it necessary that she give up the position of President of the American Red Cross. But even with the relinquishing of that responsibility her labor in behalf of others did not end, for she continued to maintain a lively interest in others until her death in 1912 at the age of ninety-one.

Clara Barton was one of the truly great American women. In founding the American Red Cross she performed a task that would insure welfare efforts in behalf of others long after she was no longer here to direct them. The Red Cross organization today is stronger than ever before, and though the future cannot be predicted with certainty, it does not seem amiss to say that it will be here, continuing its unselfish work, for many years to come.

Emma Lazarus

"Give Me Your Tired, Your Poor..."

Standing in the harbor of New York City is what is probably the world's best-known statue. It is called the Statue of Liberty. It is large, the figure itself standing 151 feet high, from the tip of the flame held high in the right hand of the Goddess of Liberty, to the base of her feet. The huge figure stands on a base that more than doubles the height of the monument, making it tower over three hundred feet above the harbor waters. It is well over 100 feet around her waist and her head is 10 feet in diameter. Twenty-five persons could easily stand inside the head without crowding; another 10 or 12 could be crowded in if necessary.

One of the most interesting things about this great colossus is the inscription that is engraved on its pedestal, a message of hope for all to see. It reads:

> "Give me your tired, your poor,
> Your huddled masses yearning to breathe free,
> The wretched refuse of your teeming shore.
> Send these, the homeless, tempest-tossed to me.
> I lift my lamp beside the golden door!"

These words change the significance of the statue for millions of people who read them. Originally intended as a token of friendship to America from France, a pledge of eternal peace between these two great nations, the statue assumes a new meaning through these words. Now it becomes a symbol of liberty for all, but especially for the humble immigrants who come to this country to seek a new life for themselves and a new hope for those who follow them.

It was a daughter of immigrants such as these who wrote the beautiful lines that are inscribed on the statue's base. Her name was Emma Lazarus and she lived in New York City. Her father had become wealthy and the family lived in very comfortable circumstances, even luxury. Emma had five sisters, but she was her father's favorite, frail and sensitive and deeply proud of her social and religious background. The family was Jewish and they were disturbed by the injustices that had been meted out to the Jews throughout their long history.

Emma lacked no material comforts, for her father indulged her every wish. She was gifted intellectually and artistically and possessed a rare beauty, though she never married. Nor is there any evidence that she ever was interested romantically with any men. She seemed content to remain at home in their large luxurious home, often not leaving it for days at a time. In the home was an extensive library which she loved, and she spent much of her time in it, reading and writing. She was a person of moods and when she was disturbed or depressed she resorted to the writing of poetry to satisfy the desires that were so strong within her.

In 1881, when Emma was thirty-two years old, there occurred an event in Europe which seemed at the time remote from any connection with her life, but which influenced her so greatly that she is remembered today almost solely because of it. Czar Alexander II of Russia was assassinated and among those who carried out the plot to slay him were a number of Jews. Seizing upon this as an excuse, the Russian police began an extensive persecution of the Jews of Russia, many of whom were killed while countless thousands of others were imprisoned or exiled to the frozen wastes of Siberia, a fate that was often worse than death. Those who were able to do so fled from Russia, many coming to the United States.

Emma Lazarus brooded over the fate of these people to whom she felt so closely tied. Newspaper accounts told of the pitiful condition of the Russian Jews when they reached New York. Most of them had fled from Russia with little except for the clothes that they wore, glad to escape with their lives. Many were ill from the long journey and the strain that they had been under. Few of them spoke English. Now they were in a strange land with a language and customs unknown to them. Bewildered and frightened, they were pitied by all who knew of their plight. Emma Lazarus knew of them and she wrote vivid articles and poems to let others know of the suffering that was going on right on our own shores.

This was not the first writing that she had done. In the seclusion of her home she had composed many poems and contributed to a number of worthy magazines. Many years before this she had sent her first little book of poetry to Ralph Waldo Emerson and he had written back to her, encouraging her in her efforts. She had contributed several excellent essays to the popular magazine, **The Century**, some of them dealing with the historical aspects of the troubles that the Jewish people had encountered down through the ages. She felt very keenly the resentment that so many people held toward her race, a feeling that very possibly contributed to her moodiness.

Because of this recognition that had come to her, Emma Lazarus was asked to write a poem that could be used to help the campaign that was then in progress to raise funds to build a suitable pedestal upon which to erect the Statue of Liberty. The statue itself was now in New York, having been shipped from France in sections in several hundred packing cases.

The design of the statue had been made by the famous French sculptor, Auguste Bartholdi. It consisted of heavy sheets of hammered copper over a huge iron framework. The actual construction of the statue was under the supervision of Gustave Eiffel, the man who a few years hence was to immortalize himself by erecting the famous tower in Paris that is even today the city's most conspicuous landmark. The work was begun in the late 1870's and completed almost five years later. Then it was dismantled and shipped to America, a gift from France to us.

There remained the problem of providing a suitable base upon which to place the 151-foot statue. No one seemed to know just where the money was to come from, for certainly it would cost a sizable sum. For some time the boxes containing the dissembled statue remained unopened. Then, aided by government officials, organizations, clubs, and individuals, efforts began to be made to secure the necessary money to build a proper pedestal.

When Emma Lazarus submitted the poem that was to be used to help solicit funds, it was immediately recognized as being something more than a mere fund-raising jingle. It was a masterly creation, deeply emotional. It changed even the purpose of the great statue from a symbol of friendship between two nations to a promise of welcome to millions of immigrants who came to America to seek a better life.

Referring to the Greek colossus which stood at the entrance to the harbor of Rhodes with one foot on each side of the harbor entrance, making it necessary for all ships entering the harbor to pass beneath the statue, Emma Lazarus wrote:

> Not like the brazen giant of Greek fame,
> With conquering limbs astride from land to land;
> Here at our sea-washed, sunset gates shall stand
> A mighty woman with a torch, whose flame
> Is the imprisoned lightning, and her name
> Mother of Exiles. From her beacon-hand
> Glows world-wide welcome; her mild eyes command
> The air-bridged harbor that twin cities frame.

Then followed the immortal lines by which she will be forever remembered:

> "Keep, ancient lands, your storied pomp!" cries she
> With silent lips. "Give me your tired, your poor,

Your huddled masses yearning to breathe free,
The wretched refuse of your teeming shore.
Send these, the homeless, tempest-tossed to me.
I lift my lamp beside the golden door."

It was June 1885, when the boxes containing the pieces of statue were unloaded in New York City. It was a year and four months later, on October 28, 1886, when the assembled monument was formally dedicated, a day never to be forgotten by those who took part in the celebration.

It was a gray day with skies overcast and a fine, cold drizzle falling. Heavy fog blanketed the harbor, making the statue and the island on which it stood in the New York harbor invisible to the people who lined the shores hoping to view the spectacular events that were transpiring.

A parade from Fifty-ninth Street formed to march down Fifth Avenue to the tip of Manhattan Island, several miles to the south. President Grover Cleveland had come to New York from Washington for the occasion. Bartholdi, the sculptor was there in the reviewing stand, and De Lesseps, digger of the Suez Canal and later to fail in the attempt to dig one across the narrow stretch of land known as Panama. There were others, many others, for it was a momentous day in our history.

There were marching bands by the score, more than a hundred of them in all, and soldiers, and many organizations, such as the Masons and the Elks, and veterans of our wars, as far back as the War of 1812, and policemen and firemen and just plain citizens. For over three hours they marched down Fifth Avenue and Broadway, then down Wall Street to the Battery.

There the land parade disbanded and the ships took over, more than three hundred of them, filled with thousands of people. There were boats of every kind and description, from rowboats to battleships; there were excursion boats and ferries; there were tugboats and yachts; and there were steamboats and sailboats, fireboats and police boats. They all had one purpose in mind, to get as close to the Statue of Liberty as possible in order to see the ceremonies that were scheduled there. The fog was thick and the drizzle persistent, so closeness was necessary.

The President's party arrived and the dedication proceedings began on schedule. Of course, in the confusion some things did go wrong. Just as the dedicatory prayer was begun by the Rev. Dr. Richard Storrs, a tugboat captain, unable to get close enough to see what was going on, let loose a blast from the boat's whistle which was quickly answered by a hundred others, completely drowning out the minister's prayer. During one of the speeches, sculptor Bartholdi, now high in the very summit of the statue, in the very torch itself, by mistake pulled the cord, which unveiled the face of Liberty and bedlam broke loose. People cheered, the whistles began anew, and the bands struck up "America." Since nobody could hear the speaker—nor cared to—he sat down with an injured air.

Finally it was all over and the boats returned their wet passengers to the shore. Under the circumstances, it was about as gala an affair as could be expected.

The words that Emma Lazarus wrote for the occasion survived that day and remain today a fitting memorial to her. They will live as long as the Statue of Liberty stands, and longer, for they stand for all that America means to the countless people from other lands who come to make their homes in this new land. Few people have a more lasting memorial.

Amelia Earhart

Pioneer of Aviation

A man who met face to face with Amelia Earhart for the first time as she stepped from her private plane expressed surprise at her appearance.

"What business has a pretty little lady like that flying alone thousands of feet up in the air?" he asked.

That was the impression that most people had of the first woman to fly alone across the Atlantic Ocean, repeating the remarkable feat of Charles Lindbergh five years earlier. Only one woman had ever flown across that ocean before and that flight occurred when Miss Earhart, accompanied by two men aviators, successfully flew from Newfoundland to Wales in 1928.

It was characteristic of Amelia Earhart to be the first in doing many things in aviation. If a challenge presented itself, she accepted it. She once flew an autogyro, ancestor of today's helicopter, across the United States, just to show that it could be done. No one knew how high the gyro would fly, so she decided to see for herself. She not only flew it higher than anyone else had flown it, but she took it up over 18,000 feet, several thousand feet higher than pilots supposedly could go without blacking out, and she did it without the use of an oxygen tank.

People have viewed her achievements in amazement and have asked, "How did Amelia Earhart ever become the remarkable person that she was?"

To seek a logical answer to this question one must go far back to her childhood days. Adults are frequently the product of the home in which they lived as children, plus the sum total of their ancestral traits. Amelia Earhart is an excellent example of the truth of this observation. Certainly her home was not a conventional one, for both her parents had ideas on child-rearing that were far ahead of their time.

Take, for example, the matter of Amelia's clothes. During the first part of this century when little girls wore stiffly starched and frilly dresses, Amelia's customary garb was a pair of blue jeans, worn at that time only by boys. And her leisure activities! Little girls just did not go fishing; rather, that was for boys to do—but Amelia did. Especially on Sunday, when most girls were dressed in their best clothes and sitting primly in Sunday school. Amelia would probably be sitting on a riverbank dressed in her blue jeans, intently watching the cork on the thin line attached to a bamboo pole. Many people were scandalized by such behavior, but it was her father who should receive the blame, if blame is to be attached to anyone.

The home-town folks in Atchison, Kansas, regarded Amelia's father as a rather unsuccessful man because he did not rise to prominence in the field of law, his chosen profession. If they were considering only the amount of money that he earned, they were probably right, for he never did earn much more than was needed to support his family. However, if one considers the wonderful way in which he taught his two daughters to live and the heritage that he passed on to them, his life was, indeed, a most successful one.

Amelia's father believed that she should do the things that she wanted to do and not always be doing something or not doing it simply because it was being done or not being done by others. Amelia liked to play baseball, so the family often played baseball together in spite of the fact that it was regarded as a boy's game by most people.

Amelia learned to throw a ball as straight as any boy could throw it. In the wintertime she and her sister went sliding on the hill together, taking a running start and then "belly-flopping" on the sled just as the boys did, although the other girls were taught to sit up straight on their sleds and be content to be pushed down the hill.

As the girls grew older, the same philosophy that guided them in early childhood continued to influence them. True, her mother taught her how to bake and cook, but at the same time her father taught her how to use a hammer and how to handle a paintbrush. Were other young girls required to be in bed by nine o'clock? Amelia could decide for herself when she thought it best to retire. If she stayed up too late one night, she would learn for herself that she would have to pay the penalty the next day by being tired and sleepy.

It was generally believed that changing schools, especially during the school year, was bad for any student. As her father moved about in his work from town to town, Amelia changed schools with considerable frequency. Instead of having a harmful effect on her, it seemed to develop in her a very desirable ability to adjust readily to a changed environment. The permissiveness that was a part of her home training tended to make her confident and self-reliant, with more poise than most girls of her age had.

Amelia attended conventional four-year high schools, six of them in all during the four years that she was in high school. She was a good student who was praised by her teachers for the quality of her work. She did not attempt to excel over other students although she very probably could have done so if she wanted to. Upon completing her high school course she enrolled in a private school in Philadelphia. She was undecided in the vocation that she would like to pursue. Very likely she would try a number of them, she said.

It was during her third year in this school that she suddenly quit in order to become a nurse's aide in a Toronto military hospital. World War I was in progress and many wounded Canadian soldiers had been sent back home from the battlefront in Europe. These men she attended for over a year without pay, content to know that she was doing a needed service. Leaving this work, she enrolled at Columbia University in New York City to begin the study of medicine. In a year she left New York to join her parents who had moved to California.

Little by little she became interested in flying. She was fascinated by the thought of being alone in a plane, thousands of feet in the air, responsible for its every movement. She decided that she must learn to fly in order to satisfy the strange longing that now seemed to fill her thoughts. One day she took her first flight, and from that moment on her interest in aviation never ceased. Although she wanted to learn to fly, the price was almost prohibitive, for her lessons would cost her a thousand dollars. To earn the needed money she took a position with the telephone company in Los Angeles, adding another job to the many that she had already tried out, only to give them up eventually for some new one with greater appeal. Her lessons went well and it wasn't long before she took her first solo flight, which proved to be the most thrilling thing that she had ever done.

Now nothing would satisfy her but owning her own plane. As usual, her parents approved of her desire and her mother helped her to finance the purchase of a small secondhand plane. When she flew it to a height of over 14,000 feet, she set a new altitude record for women, which did not seem to interest her in the least. It was the thrill of flying, and not the breaking of a record, that meant so much to her.

Amelia still had no definite preference in respect to a position that would pay her enough to permit her to fly her own plane. She accepted a position as a teacher of English, but soon left it to take a resident position with Denison House, a Boston settlement house in a poor section of the city. While there she was unexpectedly offered the opportunity to fly across the Atlantic Ocean by a publisher named George Putnam. She accepted the challenge, and in company with two men fliers she made the historic flight from Newfoundland to Wales in 1928.

The transatlantic flight catapulted her into immediate fame. In England she was feted as a heroine, and upon her return to America she was given a ticker-tape reception on Broadway such as no woman had ever received before. Her name was in every newspaper and on every tongue. The feat that she had accomplished captured everyone's imagination and all the world took her to its heart. Through it all she remained modest, even shy. The credit, she said, should be given not to her, but to the men who were in the plane with her.

She wrote magazine articles, gave lectures, made public appearances. Everywhere she went she was feted and honored. So much was her influence felt that in two years the number of licensed women pilots rose from 12 to 472. In February 1931, she married George Putnam, the publisher who was responsible for her flight across the ocean and the personal success that followed it. The next year she made her famous solo flight across the Atlantic, emulating the feat of Charles Lindbergh which had been made five years earlier. It was a dangerous trip and one that could easily have ended in disaster, but with the plane's engine aflame, she finished the journey and landed safely in Ireland. Again her name was in all headlines, on all tongues. The King of England received her to congratulate her, the French Senate awarded her the Cross of the Legion of Honor, the Belgian king and queen were her hosts. Returning to America, President and Mrs. Hoover invited her to the White House as their guest. Later, when Franklin D. Roosevelt was president, he, too, invited her to a visit at the White House and she and Mrs. Roosevelt became good friends.

Impressed with her philosophy of personal individuality, Purdue University invited her to join their staff and purchased a fine airplane for her which she flew from Hawaii to San Francisco, a distance of 2,400 miles. Then she flew it nonstop from Mexico City to Newark, New Jersey, across the river from New York City, to establish still another record. It was truly a flying laboratory in which she learned much about the effects on aviators of such factors as altitude, air pressure, fatigue, and speed.

Early in 1937 Amelia Earhart announced that she was going to fly around the world at the equator, a flying distance of about 27,000 miles. Only once had such a trip been accomplished, but that one was a much shorter one around the top of the world, a distance of about 15,000 miles. Her flight would be almost twice as long. Starting from California, she flew to Hawaii, only to crash upon taking off from the Honolulu field. Undaunted, she vowed to try again.

Two months later she did, indeed, try again, beginning the flight at Miami, Florida, stopping first in the West Indies before going on to South America, over the Atlantic to Africa, across that continent to India, from there to the East Indies and Australia and New Guinea. The longest hop of the flight lay ahead of her, and the most dangerous, for California was still seven thousand miles away and only water and islands, mere specks in the Pacific Ocean, lay between her and her homeland. Her first stop was to have been on Howland Island, a tiny bit of land near the equator. A Coast Guard cutter had been assigned to wait there to guide her in. In the ship's radio room, the crew waited tensely for word from her. It first came in the dead of night, but it was indistinguishable. An hour later, it came again, requesting help in determining her direction. Several hours went by before another contact was made.

"Our gas is running low. We must be near you but cannot see you," she said. Her voice was calm, but the strain was obvious. A half hour went by before the silence was again broken: "We cannot see you . . . we are circling . . . we cannot hear you . . ." Then only silence. That was the end.

What had happened to Amelia Earhart and her pilot? Unquestionably they had gone down somewhere in the vast Pacific, unable to locate the tiny island that was their destination. Their gasoline supply was gone; they had no alternative but to attempt a landing on the water.

A tremendous rescue operation was at once begun, but no trace of the plane was ever found. Thousands of square miles of ocean surface was covered by both ships and planes, but to no avail.

Since that day in 1937 many attempts have been made to prove that Amelia Earhart did not die in the ocean on that beautiful July morning, but that she was captured by the Japanese and imprisoned as a spy, later to die in prison. It is an improbable, fantastic story, but it is believed by many. The sensible evidence, however, is to the contrary. There is little doubt but what she died in the manner in which she had expressed a desire to go, quickly, in her plane.

Dolly Madison

White House Heroine

During the War of 1812, the British burned the White House. Living in the President's mansion at the time was James Madison and his wife Dolly. Little warning had come to them that the enemy troops were close at hand. Many rumors had been circulating recently that the British intended to burn the city. Most people gave but little credence to the rumors that were spreading, one after another. Dolly Madison herself was one who did not really believe that such a senseless thing would be done.

Then one day the word spread wildly that the British had landed and were about to burn the government buildings. Even then the courageous wife of President Madison felt in her heart that the White House would be spared.

"What would the burning of my home accomplish as far as winning the war is concerned?" she asked herself.

Men might wage war on each other, and armies fight and kill, but she could see no sense whatever in burning a defenseless home just because the President of the nation lived there. After all, it was her home, too, and in it were her furniture and her clothing and many other personal possessions that had nothing to do with war. No, she was sure that the British would spare the White House.

Her hopes were shattered when a messenger arrived from her husband, the President. "Flee at once!" the message read. "The British are on their way to burn our home!"

How did this tragic situation come about? We had won our independence from England by winning the Revolutionary War. Cornwallis had surrendered in 1781 and peace had been declared two years later. Yet, only thirty years went by before we were again at war with England and British troops were once more ravaging our countryside.

The trouble had started many years before this. In fact, although England had made peace in 1783 and had recognized our independence, it never did really respect the agreement that it had made. England was the mightiest nation in all the world in those days, while the United States was small and weak. The population of our country consisted of only a few million people, most of whom were farmers. They lived in the East, primarily, although some of the more adventurous were now seeking new homes in the region west of the Appalachian Mountains.

There were forts out there in the wilds that were still controlled by the British. In fact, the flag of England continued to float over some of the forts and trading posts that were located in territory that belonged to the United States. The Indians resented the presence of the newcomers in ever-increasing numbers and it did not take much effort on the part of the British to persuade them to attack the settlers' homes.

On the sea, matters were even worse. British ships stopped ours and sometimes forcibly took sailors from them. These unfortunate men were then made to serve in the British navy or sometimes were hanged as deserters. Several sea battles had occurred and the Americans had given a good account of themselves. In spite of promises, the British continued their unjust acts and the two nations drifted closer and closer to war.

It came in 1812 when on June 18, the United States Congress declared that a state of war existed between our country and England. There was no radio in those days nor was there a cable across the Atlantic Ocean, for if there had been, very probably there would have been no declaration of war. On June 13, five days previous to the war action taken by Congress, the British Parliament had made such concessions that would have satisfied our country sufficiently to make war unnecessary.

Dolly Payne was born in Virginia in 1768, before the Revolutionary War began. She lived on a big plantation and had a happy home life. There she grew to young girlhood. Her parents were Quakers, so Dolly, whose real name was Dorothea, though no one called her that, was reared in a very strict manner. Because she lived on a plantation, there were very few other white girls with whom to play. However, she enjoyed the associations that she had with the Negro slaves and spent many happy hours with them.

Dollys' father did not believe in slavery and eventually set all of his slaves free. Then he moved to Philadelphia where there were many Quakers. His health was poor and he died when Dolly was a young woman. She married a young lawyer named John Todd and to them two sons were born. Yellow fever broke out in the city and all four members of the family were stricken. Only Dolly and one of her boys survived; the husband, both his parents, and her baby all were victims of the dread disease.

Because her father had died penniless and her husband, too, had left her no money, Dolly and her mother opened a boarding house in Philadelphia. That city was the capital of the United States at the time and many famous people stayed with Dolly and her mother. There she met James Madison, one of the men who had helped to write the Constitution of the United States. Madison was twenty years older than Dolly, small in stature, and shy by nature. He was also brilliant, with a reputation as one of the nation's outstanding men. The two fell in love and were married in Dolly's sister's home in Virginia.

When Thomas Jefferson, who was also a Virginian, became president in 1801, he asked James Madison to be a member of his cabinet.

Jefferson's wife had died, so he asked Dolly, who was pretty, charming, and vivacious, to be the White House hostess. She agreed, and so began her many years as a society leader in the capital city. For eight years she reigned as social queen.

Then a still more wonderful thing happened to Dolly Madison. Her husband was elected President of the United States! Now she moved into the White House and for eight years more it was to be her home, with all of the exciting, gay parties that she missed so much as a Quaker girl.

Two years after war was declared, the British arrived in Washington, intent upon burning the government buildings. It was only at the last moment that Dolly Madison realized that her beloved home was to be destroyed. Her husband, the President, was out of the city, intent upon matters of importance in carrying on the war. He had left a hundred soldiers to guard the White House and to protect his wife, but when they heard that the British were coming, they fled, leaving both the mansion and its occupants unprotected.

It was at this time that Dolly showed her true mettle. A carriage was sent to the White House to take her safely away. She must hurry, the coachman said, for the British were even then on their way to burn the mansion. She looked about her, but the enemy was as yet nowhere in sight. She had treasures that could not be left behind, she said. There was the original copy of the Declaration of Independence which surely must not be destroyed. And the full-length portrait of George Washington, painted by Gilbert Stuart . . . Leave that behind? Never! Realizing that the picture, with its frame, was too large to take with her in the carriage, Dolly took a sharp knife and cut the portrait from its frame. Now she could roll it up and take it with her to safety. Only at the last moment did she yield to the coachman's frantic appeals and step into the carriage. She left much to be burned by the enemy, but her most precious treasures were saved. Today Stuart's portrait of Washington is still on view in the White House, thanks to the bravery of Dolly Madison.

When James Madison's two terms as president ended, he retired to his plantation home in Virginia. Dolly regretted giving up her exciting White House life which she had led for sixteen years. However, she found that life at Montpelier, their plantation home, was far from dull. Many people came there to pay their respects to wise James Madison and to enjoy the hospitality of his beloved wife.

For twenty years Dolly Madison was hostess to the famous people who came to Montpelier. One of them was the Marquis de Lafayette who visited America in 1824, almost a half-century after he had come here to assist us in our struggle for independence. Only once did she return to the White House and that was in the year 1835 when Andrew Jackson was president. The White House then was far from the gay place that it had been when she was mistress there.

When her husband died in 1836, Dolly Madison was once more left with hardly enough money to live on. She sold Montpelier and bought a small house in Washington where she lived quietly, though often visited by famous people. When Martin Van Buren became president, Dolly Madison became unofficial hostess once again, at the age of seventy, as the new president was a widower.

She continued active until her death. When the cornerstone of the Washington Monument was laid on July 4, 1848, she was the guest of honor. At President Polk's last White House reception she was the acknowledged queen of them all. No other American woman had ever had such a long and brilliant career, for it had covered the administrations of eleven presidents, beginning with George Washington. For almost fifty years she knew the White House intimately, figuring in its most spectacular social events.

Dolly Madison died peacefully in the winter of 1849. Few women had lived such an interesting life.

Index